Sizing Up Winter

written by

Lizann Flatt

illustrated by

Ashley Barron

FRANKLIN WATTS
LONDON•SYDNEY

Do you think that maths matters to the animals and plants?

What if nature knew numbers like you?

Let's look at winter.

Imagine what measuring could do!

When winter winds blow,
cold ice crystals grow.
High in the clouds,
is there one size for snow?

The flakes float
down,
down,
down to the ground.
How high is the snow?
How deep does it go?

How many snowflakes deep is the snow?

How far do flakes fall?
Is it one length for all?
The distance depends
on the start and the end.

How far in flakes is it for the snowy owl
to fly from one perch to the other?

Could cardinals and chickadees
demand all their seeds
from feeders of a certain size?

How many birds long
is each feeder? Are the
feeders the same size?

Do the deer mice mind that a snowshoe hare
takes far fewer steps to get its food over there?

How many footprints long is the
distance for the deer mouse?
For the snowshoe hare?

When the snow fleas flip-flop and pop on the snow,
would they fit themselves into neat columns and rows?

How many snow fleas cover
the area of this sunny space?

When sliding into place,
might otters measure space?

How many otters fit into each lake?
Which lake has a larger capacity?

Would a mother polar bear
use her babies to compare?

Which has more mass, the mother or her cubs?

Could the porcupine pile its leftovers each day
so the pine piles show all the days gone away?

According to the piles, how many days have passed?
How else could you describe that length of time?

Might a herd of musk oxen create an analog clock when the ptarmigan asks for the time?

Does the musk ox clock show 7:00 a.m., 12:15 p.m., or 8:00 p.m.? Would you call this breakfast time, lunchtime, or bedtime?

Underneath the ice, the water's fairly nice.
Could the creatures compare?
Hold a contest? Would they dare?

Which turtle is tallest?

Which frog is fattest?

Which trout is tiniest?

Which bass is biggest?

Which ling is longest?

Would a week be something
a weasel would know?
Would it know if one week meant
its white fur would go?

**Can you put the days in order as
the weasel's fur turns from white
to brown? Can you give a name to
each day of the weasel's week?**

When groundhogs wait,
or hibernate,
would they track their
wake-up date?

Which date is circled on the
calendar? Which months did
the groundhog sleep through?

NOVEMBER

DECEMBER

JANUARY

So how long is winter, and how do you know?
Is it winter as long as it's cold and there's snow?
When will winter be over? What day will it go?
Will it end with a colourful nighttime light show?

Which months are winter for you?

Is winter always frozen?
Is winter always cold?
Think about where you live.
What does your winter hold?

What's winter like
where you live?

So ... does nature know numbers?
No way! That's not true.
The only creatures to need numbers?
Actually, just you.

Nature Notes

The **snowy owl** is different from most other owls because it is active during the day. It lives in cold northern regions, even as high as the Arctic tundra. When hunting, it makes use of its excellent hearing to find prey under the snow. Snowy owls can eat up to five lemmings a day.

In winter, **northern cardinals** gather in large flocks. They eat mostly seeds and fruit, often at backyard bird feeders. **Black-capped chickadees** will swoop into a bird feeder, take a seed, and fly away. They prefer to hide seeds and other food to eat later. They live in flocks and often mingle with other types of birds.

In North America, **Deer mice** store seeds in places like holes in trees. During the winter nights, they visit their saved seeds and look for other food. A **snowshoe hare**'s large back feet are covered with extra fur. These fluffy hind feet help the hare stay on top of the snow. Both animals often leave footprints in the snow.

Snow fleas, also called springtails, live in moist places. They are easy to see on sunny winter days near the bases of trees. A special body part on their underside, called a furcula, flicks down on the snow or ground and pops or "springs" the snow flea up into the air!

River otters like to play. They slide on their bellies down hills during winter and summer, and wrestle and splash in the water. They have webbed back feet to help them swim, and they can close their nostrils and ears to keep out water.

In the Arctic, a female **polar bear** digs a den in a snowbank around mid-October. Her cubs, usually twins, are born inside the den. Through the long winter, the cubs drink their mother's milk, but the mother doesn't eat anything. All three come out of the den in March or April.

Evergreen trees such as hemlocks, pines, and spruces keep their needles all winter. The needles have a waxy coating to reduce moisture loss in dry winter air. At night the **North American porcupine** will climb these trees to eat the inner bark, twigs, and needles, often making trails in the snow from its den to its favorite food trees.

If **musk oxen** feel threatened, they will bunch up in a group with their backsides together and their heads facing out. **Willow ptarmigans**, also known as willow grouses, turn mostly white in winter. Their feet are covered in feathers during winter and act like snowshoes. Both musk oxen and ptarmigans live in the Arctic.

As a lake freezes over, fish like **bass** and **trout** move and eat less and less. **Ling**, or burbot, live near the bottom of lakes. They lay eggs under the ice in shallow water. **Snapping turtles** bury themselves in the mud at the bottom of a lake to hibernate. **Northern leopard frogs** also hibernate under water, but they sit on top of or only partly buried in the mud.

In winter, **weasels** have white fur, but it's brown the rest of the year. They hunt voles and deer mice all winter, and will even store these animals to eat later when hunting is not so good. A weasel lines its den with grasses, leaves — and even fur from its prey!

A **groundhog** is also called a woodchuck. During winter, it curls up in its burrow underground and hibernates. During hibernation, its heartbeat slows down to only four or five beats a minute, and it doesn't eat at all until spring. Groundhogs live in the USA and Canada.

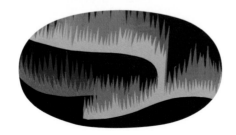

Green and red or blue bands of light in the sky are called the **northern lights**, or aurora borealis. These lights are made when energy from the sun reacts with the Earth's atmosphere. One of the best times to see the northern lights is when winter turns to spring.

To Kiera, who always more than measures up.
Let your dreams tip the scales with their size.
  ~Lizann

For my sister, Jennifer, and all of her students
in Pangnirtung, Nunavut.
  ~Ashley

Text © 2013 Lizann Flatt
Illustrations © 2013 Ashley Barron

Franklin Watts
First published in Great Britain in 2017 by The Watts Publishing Group

Text © 2012 Lizann Flatt
Illustrations © 2012 Ashley Barron
Design: Claudia Dávila

Published by permission of Owlkids Books Inc., Toronto, Ontario, Canada.

ISBN 978 1 4451 5779 5

Printed in China

Franklin Watts
An imprint of Hachette Children's Group
Part of the Watts Publishing Group
Carmelite House
50 Victoria Embankment
London EC4Y 0DZ

An Hachette UK Company
www.hachette.co.uk

www.franklinwatts.co.uk

MIX
Paper from
responsible sources
FSC® C104740
FSC
www.fsc.org

CANCELLED